Hair

For Ella and Bella

First published in North America in 2006 by Two-Can Publishing
11571 K-Tel Drive, Minnetonka, MN 55343
www.two-canpublishing.com

A portion of the proceeds from this book will benefit Oxfam GB.

Oxfam would like to acknowledge, with thanks, the following photographers:
Annie Bungeroth (pages 6–7), Marj Clayton (pages 22–23), Howard Davies (pages 5 and 26–27),
Sarah Errington (pages 12–13 and cover), Jim Holmes (pages 10–11), Ley Honor Roberts (pages 14–15),
Crispin Hughes (pages 18–19 and 24–25), Philippe Lissac (pages 16–17)
Rajendra Shaw (pages 20–21 and back cover) and Sean Sprague (pages 8–9).
The book begins on page 6.

First published in Great Britain in 2006 by Frances Lincoln Children's Books
4 Torriano Mews, Torriano Avenue, London NW5 2RZ
www.franceslincoln.com

Library of Congress Cataloging-in-Publication Data on file

ISBN 1-58728-531-2 (HC)
ISBN 1-58728-532-0 (PB)

Printed in China

1 2 3 4 5 10 09 08 07 06

Hair

Kate Petty

 in association with Oxfam

It is cold in the high mountains of Pakistan. Pedan and Samullah have thick, dark hair. It is cut short so it doesn't get in their eyes.

My hat keeps my head warm.

Ana is combing Maria's hair outside their home in Guatemala. She is going to tie it back with a red scrunchie.

I want to look like my big sister.

Linh lives in Vietnam.
He is washing his hair at
the well outside his house
before he goes to school.

It's hard to wash just my hair!

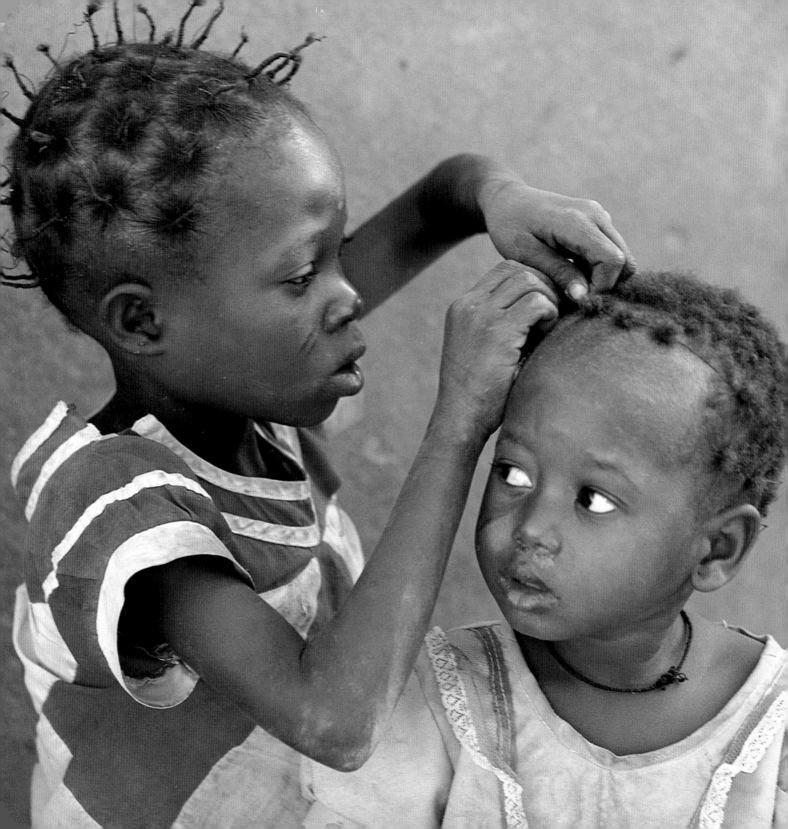

Felicia and Anongee are friends.
They live in Ghana. Felicia parts
Anongee's curls into neat rows.
Then she ties them into
little clumps.

I have to sit
very still.

Martha likes to make her sister Ruby look pretty. She has picked some flowers from their garden in the United States.

This pink flower is my favorite.

Doesn't Catherine look beautiful with yellow beads in her braids? She lives in a small African country called Togo.

The beads feel nice when I shake my head.

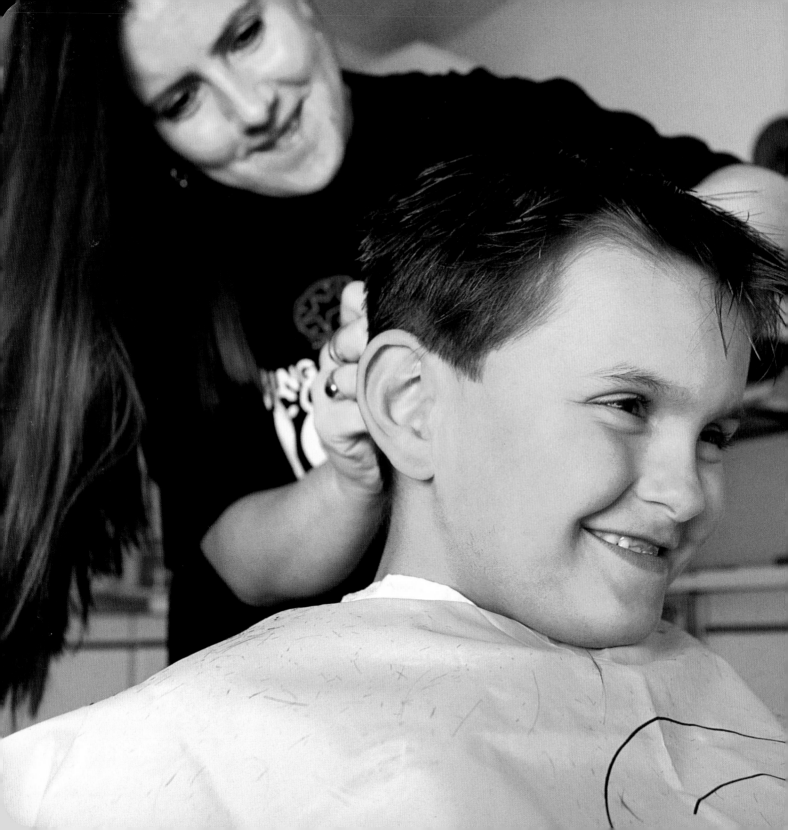

Nathaneal is getting his hair cut at home in the United Kingdom. He uses gel to make it stand up.

I like my hair to look cool!

Shakeel lives in India. He wants to look neat for the festival today. He has put oil in his hair to keep it in place. The oil is scented with spices.

My hair oil smells nice in the hot sun.

Liliana must have some of the longest braids in the world! She lives in one of the highest cities in the world, too: La Paz, Bolivia.

I tie back my braids when I am working.

Wolo's friends have fixed her hair.
This style from Burkina Faso
shows off her pretty earrings.

Wires help
my spiky hair
to stay up!

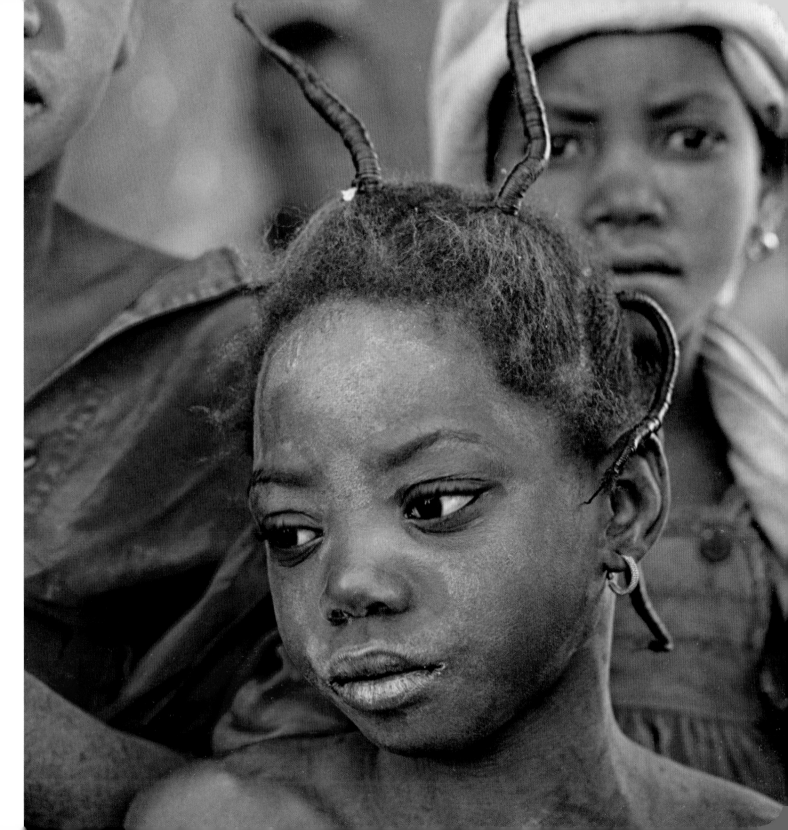

Kim lives in a village in Cambodia called Prek Chdoar. She has long hair, which she likes to wear loose.

I can tie my hair back if it gets too hot.

United States

United Kingdom

Guatemala

Burkina Faso

Ghana

Togo

Bolivia

Pakistan

India

Vietnam

Cambodia